THE COMPANION DEVOTIONAL JOURNAL

Planted By Water

DEEPENING YOUR SPIRITUAL
CONNECTEDNESS TO GOD

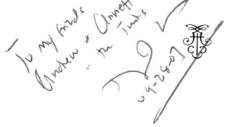

DEVON ANTHONY BLACKWOOD

Cold Tree Press

Cover Photo by Richard Collier © 2005
To see more of Richard Collier's work please visit his web site at:
www.richardcollierphotography.com

Author Photo by
Cameo Studio of Photography & Video Productions
9333 Belair Road, Perry Hall, MD 21236
410-256-3320

Poetry Credits:
"In Thine Heart" by Emma Loftus
"A Fork In The Road" by Hannah Loftus

All quotes and after thoughts by Devon A. Blackwood

Published by Cold Tree Press
Nashville, Tennessee
www.coldtreepress.com

Dedication

This book is warmly dedicated to:

My Father
Calvin James Blackwood
Dad has gone on (May 26, 2004) to be with the Lord
but his memories live warmly in our hearts.

&

My Mother
Romency Blackwood
Mom is a tireless worker for God who stays planted when
times are hard, and who has genuine compassion
and kindness in her heart for everyone she meets.

&

My Wife
Rosemarie "Jackie" Blackwood
Rosemarie is my number one supporter, motivator,
and friend for life.

THE COMPANION DEVOTIONAL JOURNAL

Planted By Water

DEEPENING YOUR SPIRITUAL
CONNECTEDNESS TO GOD

DEVON ANTHONY BLACKWOOD

Chapter 1
Dehydration: Running Dry

*Preparation is a priceless principle; man's
very survival depends on it.*

We care for our physical body by ingesting the right
nourishment and water. We stay healthy when we do so.
How are you caring for your spiritual soul?

_____

_____

_____

_____

_____

_____

_____

_____

_____

_____

_____

What are your plans to improve and strengthen
your prayer life?

_____

_____

_____

_____

_____

_____

_____

_____

_____

_____

Are you committed or effective in your fasting?
Why or why not?

_____

_____

_____

_____

_____

_____

_____

_____

_____

_____

_____

_____

Make a list of individuals you can rely on
to strengthen your walk in Christ.

_____

_____

_____

_____

_____

_____

_____

_____

_____

_____

_____

How will you stay spiritually hydrated? Be specific.

_____

_____

_____

_____

_____

_____

_____

_____

_____

_____

_____

_____

Your reflective moment.

_____

_____

_____

_____

_____

_____

Meditative Verse

Therefore we do not lose heart even though our outward man is perishing, yet the Inward man is being renewed day by day.

—II Corinthians 4:16

After Thought

Prayer is the key that comforts the heart and it gives renewed strength to endure the challenge ahead of us.

Chapter 2
Purity: Standing Above Ground

Whatever thoughts fill our minds also influence our Lives.
They share our words and dictate our interactions with others.

Many things can distract us from living pure.
What are your specific distractions or challenges?

_____

_____

_____

_____

_____

_____

_____

_____

_____

_____

_____

_____

What are your intentions to overcome these battles?

_____

_____

_____

_____

_____

_____

_____

_____

_____

Who will help you succeed?

_____

_____

_____

_____

_____

_____

_____

_____

_____

_____

_____

_____

_____

How will you filter out, or keep Satan
out, of your personal space?

_____

_____

_____

_____

_____

_____

_____

_____

_____

_____

_____

List your strengths and identify how you will use
them to keep a clean sanctuary.

_____

_____

_____

_____

_____

_____

_____

_____

Your reflective moment.

_____

_____

_____

_____

_____

_____

_____

_____

_____

_____

_____

_____

_____

_____

_____

_____

_____

_____

_____

_____

_____

_____

_____

_____

_____

_____

_____

_____

_____

_____

_____

Meditative Verse

Search me, O God, and know my heart; Try me,
and know my anxieties; And see if there is any wicked
way in me, And lead me in the way everlasting.

—Psalm 139:23-24

After Thought

If we struggle with sin, we must continually submit it to God,
and let our hearts become fertile ground for His work in our lives.

Chapter 3
Word of Mouth: A Day in the Life of an Evangelist

It has been said that the greatest sermon you will ever preach is the life you live.

Often, fear or intimidation keep us from sharing the Good news of Salvation. What are your specific fears?

_____

_____

_____

_____

_____

_____

_____

_____

_____

_____

_____

_____

How will you conquer them?

_____

_____

_____

_____

_____

_____

_____

_____

_____

Describe the things you're passionate about.
Do these things relate to witnessing and evangelism?
If not, do you have a desire to witness and evangelize?

_____

_____

_____

_____

_____

_____

_____

_____

_____

_____

_____

_____

_____

_____

_____

_____

_____

What admirable qualities do you possess
that can help lead others to Christ?

_____

_____

_____

_____

_____

_____

_____

_____

_____

_____

_____

_____

_____

What are your plans to communicate the gospel?
Who can you team up with to win souls?

_____

_____

_____

_____

_____

_____

_____

_____

_____

_____

_____

_____

_____

_____

Your reflective moment.

_____

_____

_____

_____

_____

_____

_____

_____

_____

_____

_____

_____

_____

_____

Meditative Verse

The law of the Lord is perfect, converting the soul;
The testimony of the Lord is sure, making wise the simple.

—Psalm 19:7

After Thought

God is more interested in doers, action-oriented folks,
than those who say they will do, but do not.

Chapter 4
Rocky Terrain: The Trials of Job, Joseph and Paul

We are not always privy to see what God sees;
He only wants us to follow Him along the paths He takes us
and trust Him completely along the way.

Test and trials are a big part of our lives.
What are your specific trials?

_____

_____

_____

_____

_____

_____

_____

_____

_____

_____

_____

What are your perspectives towards them?
Are you maturing and growing in the Word?

_____

_____

_____

_____

_____

_____

_____

_____

Problems can strain us emotionally.
How do you cope with distress in your life?

_____

_____

_____

_____

_____

_____

_____

_____

_____

_____

_____

_____

_____

_____

_____

Who can you rely on to help you in tough times?

_____

_____

_____

_____

_____

_____

_____

_____

_____

_____

_____

What are your God-allowed trials?
What are your self-induced trials?

_____

_____

_____

_____

_____

_____

_____

_____

_____

_____

_____

Your reflective moment.

_____

_____

_____

_____

_____

_____

_____

_____

_____

_____

_____

_____

_____

_____

_____

_____

_____

_____

_____

_____

_____

_____

_____

_____

_____

_____

_____

_____

Meditative Verse

God is our refuge and strength,
a very present help in trouble.

—Psalm 46:1

After Thought

To get through trials one must wholeheartedly believe that the Lord
is our strength and shield, our way maker and our great deliverer.

Chapter 5
The Fighting Soul

*We need not fear the battle for God has given us
the Spirit of power (Holy Spirit Power) to speak to
the mountain that stands in our way.*

War, whether spiritual or physical can be brutal.
What is the spiritual warfare in your life?

_____

_____

_____

_____

_____

_____

_____

_____

_____

_____

_____

_____

How can you defeat the enemy's devices?

_____

_____

_____

_____

_____

_____

_____

_____

_____

_____

_____

_____

What is your AP (alert plan) and is it in place?

_____

_____

_____

_____

_____

_____

_____

_____

_____

_____

_____

_____

_____

_____

_____

Sometimes our oil is low or our lamp power has
completely faded. What are your plans to avoid this?

_____

_____

_____

_____

_____

_____

_____

_____

_____

_____

_____

_____

_____

_____

_____

_____

_____

_____

_____

Do you give up easily? Why or why not?

_____

_____

_____

_____

_____

_____

_____

_____

_____

_____

Your reflective moment.

Meditative Verse

The Lord is on my side; I will not fear.
What can man do to me?

—Psalm 118:6

After Thought

Putting aside self-reliance is prudent when it comes to
hearing God's voice. He is the leader in battle, knows the
ins and outs, and will take us to victory.

Chapter 6
The Wait: Your Calling,
Your Gifts

We are not here to glorify our bodies or our minds or our works,
but to fulfill God's purpose here on earth.

What God endowed gifts have you received and
are you working in them?

_____

_____

_____

_____

_____

_____

_____

_____

_____

_____

_____

_____

If you struggle with feelings of inferiority or inadequacy,
how will you bring about resolution?

_____

_____

_____

_____

_____

_____

_____

_____

_____

How can you maximize your gifts to edify your local
church and God's kingdom at large?

_____

_____

_____

_____

_____

_____

_____

Your reflective moment.

Meditative Verse

Therefore, having these promises, beloved, let us cleanse ourselves from all filthiness of the flesh and spirit, perfecting holiness in the fear of God.

—II Corinthians 7:1

After Thought

We must remember that spiritual gifts are not about us; they are about God and the furtherance of His kingdom here on earth.

Chapter 7
Repairing The Heart

If we are honest enough to admit it, we all have pain.
At one time or another, we have all cried inside.

So often, we live with despair and distress that strains our Spiritual life. What things weigh you down?

_____

_____

_____

_____

_____

_____

_____

_____

_____

_____

_____

_____

_____

How will you rectify these conditions?

_____

_____

_____

_____

_____

_____

_____

_____

_____

_____

_____

_____

Are your emotions clogged up or bogged down with debris?
If so, what steps will you take to find healing?

_____

_____

_____

_____

_____

_____

Who do you trust enough to help you with your endeavor?

_____

Your reflective moment.

Meditative Verse

I will lift up my eyes to the hills from whence comes my help.
My help comes from the Lord, who made heaven and earth.

—Psalm 121:1

After Thought

It is not hurt that holds us back, it is our fear
or reluctance to turn it over to God.

Chapter 8
The Conquered Wall

It seems like the hardest thing in the world to do is to forgive, but forgiveness is an authentic and true test of our Christian character.

What's written on the pages of your heart?

_____

_____

_____

_____

_____

_____

_____

_____

_____

_____

_____

_____

_____

_____

————————————————

————————————————

————————————————

————————————————

Perhaps you've suffered a recent hurt or betrayal.
How will you heal?

————————————————

————————————————

————————————————

————————————————

————————————————

————————————————

————————————————

————————————————

————————————————

————————————————

————————————————

————————————————

————————————————

————————————————

What do you think contributed or caused this situation and how have you dealt with it?

_____

_____

_____

_____

_____

_____

_____

_____

_____

_____

_____

_____

_____

_____

So far, has forgiveness been easy or a struggle?

_____

_____

_____

_____

_____

_____

Do you intend to reach out to those who have caused you grief?
If so, what are your plans?

_____

_____

_____

_____

_____

_____

_____

_____

_____

_____

_____

_____

_____

_____

_____

_____

_____

Your reflective moment.

_____

_____

_____

_____

_____

_____

_____

_____

_____

_____

_____

_____

_____

_____

_____

_____

_____

_____

_____

_____

Meditative Verse

*And we have known and believed the love that God
has for us. God is love, and he who abides in
love abides in God, and God in him.*

—I John 4:16

After Thought

*When we show others forgiveness,
it sends a powerful message of hope. In the midst of darkness,
forgiveness gives them light.*

Chapter 9
Seeds That Poison

*If we keep poisonous seeds out of our lives
we won't have to fret about being soiled, but bad seeds seem to keep
sprouting, cropping up all around us.*

If God took inventory of your spiritual walk
what would He find?

_____

_____

_____

_____

_____

_____

_____

_____

_____

_____

_____

_____

_____

_____

_____

_____

_____

_____

_____

_____

_____

Are you happy with your reputation? Why or why not?

_____

_____

_____

_____

_____

_____

_____

_____

_____

_____

_____

_____

_____

_____

_____

_____

_____

Do works of the flesh mar your character? If so, describe them.
What steps will you take to rid your life of poisonous seeds?

_____

_____

_____

_____

_____

_____

_____

_____

_____

_____

_____

_____

_____

Your reflective moment.

Meditative Verse

With my soul I have desired you in the night, yes, by my spirit within me I will seek you early; for when your judgments are in the earth, the inhabitants of the world will learn righteousness.

—Isaiah 26:9

After Thought

When we are filled with the Spirit of Christ and walking in His Word, the devil will have no power to influence us with his earthly wine.

Chapter 10
Faith: A Walk On The Wild Side

*If you are serious about putting your faith to the test,
it shouldn't be tested when the sea is calm, but when it
is stirred up.*

Faith is an essential part of being a Christian.
Describe your faith. Is it weak or is it strong?

_____

_____

_____

_____

_____

_____

_____

_____

_____

_____

_____

_____

_____

_____

_____

_____

_____

_____

_____

_____

_____

What are some supernatural things that God has done for you?

_____

_____

_____

_____

_____

_____

_____

_____

_____

How can your faith increase?

_____

_____

_____

_____

_____

_____

_____

_____

_____

_____

_____

_____

_____

_____

_____

What lessons can you take from Peter's walk on water?

_____

_____

_____

_____

_____

_____

_____

_____

_____

_____

_____

_____

_____   .

_____

Your reflective moment.

_____

_____

_____

_____

_____

_____

_____

_____

_____

Meditative Verse

*I have come as a light into the world, that whoever believes
in me should not abide in darkness.*

—John 12:46

After Thought

*To be effective Christians, we must never allow even
our best friend to impede our step of faith.*

Chapter 11
Foundations of Family

You cannot communicate to Heaven,
if those on earth you ignore.

Quiet moments with God build relationship.
Do you spend quality time seeking Him? Elaborate.

_____

_____

_____

_____

_____

_____

_____

_____

_____

_____

_____

_____

_____

_____

_____

_____

_____

_____

_____

_____

_____

God is already aware of all your needs and desires.
How will you wait on Him to supply them?

_____

_____

_____

_____

_____

_____

_____

_____

_____

_____

_____

_____

If you're married or single your struggles might still be the same. How will you ward off things like lust or sexual sins?

_____

_____

_____

_____

_____

_____

_____

_____

_____

_____

_____

_____

_____

Think about your personal desires. Do you think you will receive them? Why or why not?

_____

_____

_____

_____

_____

Your reflective moment.

_____
_____
_____
_____
_____
_____
_____
_____
_____
_____
_____
_____
_____
_____
_____
_____
_____
_____
_____
_____
_____
_____
_____

Meditative Verse

*Remember now your Creator in the days of your youth,
before the difficult days come, and the years draw near when you
say, I have no pleasure in them.*

—Ecclesiastes 12:1

After Thought

Welcome God in your home then reap the good things in store.

Chapter 12
Mother's Prayers

You can use an umbrella to keep you dry in the rain,
but it is prayer that covers you in storms.

What is it that you want your friends, coworkers,
and/or your children to know about God?

_____

_____

_____

_____

_____

_____

_____

_____

_____

_____

_____

_____

_____

_____

How will you convey this message?

_____

_____

_____

_____

_____

_____

_____

_____

_____

_____

_____

Describe a well-balanced life with the key
Ingredients it needs.

_____

_____

_____

_____

_____

_____

_____

_____

_____

_____

_____

Is your life spiritually balanced? Elaborate.

_____

_____

_____

_____

_____

_____

_____

_____

_____

_____

_____

_____

Your reflective moment.

Meditative Verse

The Lord is good, A stronghold in the day of trouble;
and He knows those who trust in Him.

—Nahum 1:7

After Thought

The weapons of Satan cannot harm you if you're
hidden in Almighty God.

Chapter 13
Fruit of the Spirit

If we are committed to setting our foundation on good soil and planting good seeds, we will bear good fruit.

God is committed to ridding our lives of bad fruit.
What bad fruit are you weeding out?

_____

_____

_____

_____

_____

_____

_____

_____

_____

_____

_____

_____

_____

_____

What do you need more of and how will you achieve it?

_____

_____

_____

_____

_____

_____

_____

_____

_____

What do you think about the following attributes?
How are they applicable to your life and to others?

Love

_____

_____

_____

_____

_____

_____

_____

_____

_____

_____

_____

Joy

_____

_____

_____

_____

_____

_____

_____

_____

_____

_____

Peace

_____

_____

_____

_____

_____

———————————————

———————————————

———————————————

———————————————

———————————————

Longsuffering

———————————————

———————————————

———————————————

———————————————

———————————————

———————————————

———————————————

———————————————

———————————————

———————————————

Kindness

———————————————

———————————————

———————————————

_____

_____

_____

_____

_____

_____

_____

_____

Goodness

_____

_____

_____

_____

_____

_____

_____

_____

_____

_____

_____

_____

Faithfulness

_____

_____

_____

_____

_____

_____

_____

_____

_____

_____

Gentleness

_____

_____

_____

_____

_____

_____

_____

_____

_____

_____

Self-control

_____

_____

_____

_____

_____

_____

_____

_____

_____

_____

Write about a person in whom the fruit of the Spirit shines.
How has this person impacted your life?

_____

_____

_____

_____

_____

_____

_____

_____

_____

_____

_____

_____

_____

_____

_____

_____

_____

_____

_____

_____

_____

_____

_____

_____

_____

_____

_____

_____

Your reflective moment.

Meditative Verse

*Whoever walks blamelessly will be saved, but he who is
perverse in his ways will suddenly fall.*

—Proverbs 28:18

After Thought

*Just because we are exposed to sinful living doesn't
automatically mean we cannot change, or that we must die in it.*

Chapter 14
The Benediction

His grace sustains us as we leave personal tragedies,
discouragement, and failures behind.

What personal tragedies have you suffered
and how have you coped so far?

_____

_____

_____

_____

_____

_____

_____

_____

_____

_____

_____

_____

_____

_____

_____

_____

_____

_____

_____

Discouragement is a part of life.
How will you keep a good attitude?

_____

_____

_____

_____

_____

_____

_____

_____

_____

_____

_____

_____

_____

_____

Have you ever run in a marathon or a track meet?
How did you prepare?

_____

_____

_____

_____

_____

_____

_____

Did you aim to win? Why or why not?

_____

_____

_____

_____

_____

_____

_____

_____

_____

_____

What do you hope to achieve in your spiritual walk?

_____

_____

_____

_____

_____

_____

_____

_____

You've stayed in the race to the finish line. How do you feel?
What rewards are in store?

_____

_____

_____

_____

_____

_____

_____

_____

_____

_____

_____

_____

_____

Your reflective moment.

_____

_____

_____

_____

_____

_____

_____

_____

_____

_____

_____

_____

_____

Meditative Verse

When He had called the people to Himself, with His disciples also,
He said to them, "Whoever desires to come after Me, let him
deny himself, and take up his cross, and follow Me."

—Mark 8:34

After Thought

When everything stops and the moment of reckoning comes,
he who holds on to Heaven's roadmap will cross the finish line.

In Thine Heart

In thine heart there is a place,
Where merely one may tread,
If, per chance, thee let Him in,
He takes thine idols stead.
This place had beauty,
Beyond all thought,
To keep it pure, how hard He's fought,
'Tis Jesus' home, 'tis His duty,
All in all, 'tis His beauty.

—Emma Loftus, Age 14

A Fork in the Road

When one is walking on the trail of life,
He comes to a fork in the road,
One road is full of strife,
The other is calm and peaceful,
One road is Hell,
The other is Heaven,
Where all your things you must sell,
So now take your choice,
Do you wish to raise your voice to Him,
Or live with evil and their kin,
Shall you thank Him for taking your sin?

—Hannah Loftus, Age 10

About the Author

Devon Anthony Blackwood is an administrator, education director, and teacher at the Shiloh Church of God Seventh Day in Baltimore, Maryland. Author of *Beyond The Lingo*, he counsels in the Psychiatry department at Johns Hopkins Hospital and is President & CEO of B.W. Affiliates, LLC, a mental health and consulting firm. He has traveled extensively on mission trips and lectured in many parts of the world including the United States of America, South America, Europe, Africa, and the Caribbean.

In his spare time, Devon enjoys playing the guitar and piano, reading, mentoring youth, and writing. He also enjoys spending time with his wife, Rosemarie, and the joy of his life, Kate-Lynn, age 4. He holds a psychology degree from the University of Baltimore.

Printed in the United States
77439LV00003B/340-348